Is It Easy To Be Alive?

Thomas Marston

Presentation by *BookLeaf Publishing*

Web: www.bookleafpub.com

E-mail: info@bookleafpub.com

ISBN: 978-93-95755-72-6

First edition 2022

To those who make it easier.

Piss Wagon

Mount high,
mountain low
mount and conquer
this hoe.

Dick-wagon express
for a dethroned empress,
talk too much
and die,
think too much
and end.

Piss Wagon.
In the end
I'm a piss wagon
lacking tires,
a piss wagon
forever tired,
weary of nothing
but lightless fires.

Am I sad,
or do I just want to be?
Is this who I am,
or is it just poetry?
To die is to live

in pity's eternity.
Taken of your own,
the martyr
kills himself
hopefully.

Only the Insane are Free?

I ask my self,
am I in touch
with myself?

What is everyone selling,
what have I bought?
Is there any me left?
Anything left of Anything?

What am I?
A mosaic a collage a gruel
of every idea anyone's had
who spoke to me?

Is that all I am,
all I could be?
A collection of words?
Further,
must I be more?

Long Rope

One drink too many
and twenty too few:
go to sleep now
and lay it down.

Vodka sings with a voice
her own,
beer and rum do too,
these well-worn towns.

Where concrete dreams
and oil burns
and crickets laugh
and tables turn.

CLR

Brush your teeth
with calcified rot.

Wash your hands
of uncleanly thought.

I wish I knew
wound's deepest peace,

blessed piss
and my self-harm plot.

Give me nothing
but an endless draught

all naught and
guilt's spilled grease.

Two Ponds At Sunset

Two ponds at sunset,
orange sun and purple haze,
a black bird sings
at end of days.

Wandered far,
but not far enough,
return to my boat
and broken oars.

Swimming up we swim beyond
to nights of dreams and unrealities.
Come with me, come with me
atop two ponds at sunset

through the black-bird song
and into the end of days.

Round 1

Hey.
Bull-faced,
in that white lace,
wander over to my place.

Drawn on eyebrows
maybe a nice face,
ruined by tears
and wrinkles and the sun.

And I know it's hard,
what you've done,
this listless race
over-top pace
run until your feet give out
a horny nun
china-shop terror
fuck it don't need your love,
parody, hypocrisy,
eternally,
internally.

Internal's the only place we live.
Inside, run on
the walls,

tear them down
build them stronger:
loveless fools
kiss the same.

Don't struggle,
you're wrong either way,
so die trying,
crying
blood.

To Poets

A

watered down
existence
lived only by words.

What do you
do it for?
Just so there's more?

Round 2

Flower pot lover,
soup kitchen smuggler,
old man revolt,
stomach pains in my gut.

The rain's coming down
in drifting piano tunes and
I sound other times and
lend life a snack, a smoke,
a light and
a light.

Mirror crash broken

who are we and
is this life?

Sell my pills
sell me pills,
back to life love
thrust push rush
wander fingers
over us
dripping spit
and glass cum.

Fly on,
buzz-boy.
Find another
piece of shit.

I am mine,
and
atleast I'm
mine,

not like those petals and the sun
shared by everyone,
fuck love,
all that I've had,
or ever will.

I like my meat overdone.

Sweet Honey Silence

I'm tired of all the voices
yelling laughing joking
little sarcasms and wistless
wit and all the thinking,
all pre-doing.
I'm tired of the noise
and the grey roaring echo
thudding down overpacked corridors,
I'm tired.

Round 3

There's a little song playing
and I'm all alone writing
sinful poems and saying
nothing new, but grinning.

I'm skinning rotten cows
for broken hooves and nuts,
replacing my nails, eyebrows
with sacred scapegoat cuts.

Strung up on the mountain
chained to great boulders unrolling,
after rolling, crying, breaking,
laying down with my weary pen bleeding.

Is it easy or not hard enough:
what's living without a death-rush?

Well, Brother?

Do you have the spirit?
Do you have the flames?
Rush rush rush
far out and find them:
there is nothing else.
I will help you,
my friend,
and we will rush sea to sea
to frozen sea
for the spirit and the flames
and we will live on nothing
until we do.
Rush!
Screaming,
rush!
Dare yearn tear drown,
rush,
step out and live,
decide
and
rush!

If there is no spirit,
there can be nothing!

So, my brother,
we must find it.
So if we don't have it,
we must,
together,
straining,
rush.

Pen Wise

Pen-wise glory
given edge
to the fuller
of my two
outlets.

Oh pen
o' mine,
oh mine,
most sacred piece.

Divine,
Oh write
divine,
post-office tantrum like
send bombs in the mail
bombed as a male
oh light of mine
oh light, oh mine,

another spark.

Big Old Fuckers

Fuck the rhymes
and fuck your truth.
Give me lies,
they're just the same,
so long as they're in verse
I'll love all that shit,
a love-sick mongrel.

Oh well.
Am I?
Do I want to be?
Do I live
or emulate?

Am who I am
and do I love
what I love?
Am I just sorrow
in a rum-filled glass?

Do I cry
or perform?

Hey fucker?
Stroke my hair

and I'll tell you
how I tried to cheat
in my naivety
guilt
hatred.

An Apartment Hot and Humid

An apartment hot and humid
fans and open windows and sirens
and half naked lovers
laughing in the shadows.

Streetlamps, Back Parking Lot

An orange light brightly burns
from the parking lot pole,
burnt and dark and solemn.
To it, the shadows yearn.

Grasping at the night
breaking the silence below,
a man goes wandering
screaming for some night.

Echo Call

Something I had,
I'll get it back
in my heart's deep pit
I feel the echo call
of desire,
of need,
of flame-fold desperation,
burning.

Whitebread Overbite

This gaping maw,
I wish I could devour
the world
swallow life whole
chew through being
doing the utmost to
shit the entirety
in its whole.
Let lies fall from your mouth
unchewed crumbs are as good
as anything else.

Lies are the spice
of life,
dearer than a feast of truths,
spit out everything
and give up nothing.

In Bloom, Dead Flowers

Dispossessed of life,
I'll find my worth in words.

An author,
nothing else.
A ghost in life:
how can it be used,
boiled down into
insignificant words
and fail
to capture the everything
I saw and experienced
but now never lived.

Maybe next time,
we'll live
maybe next time
and maybe the next one
is it.
But it's all nothing
to me.

Cry Then

Cry if it makes
you feel better.
Tears wash no pain
paint no canvases
draw no words
and ideas aren't held
in those refracting
droplets of
life, light.

Or, give it nothing
forget,
and go back to work.

Make your choice.

A Siren

A lonely siren wails
echoing in concrete mazes.

Distant it sings,
the entirety of someone's life.

Wail, wail, wail,
oh, for the dying,

grasp out tearing
for something solid back,

echo and fade
all over again.

Oh it sings, asking,
are you comfortable?

A Little Pink Heart

I sat in my apartment
with an empty hole
thinking or dreaming
it wasn't there.

The night was hot
humid and cold,
and I drank and I drank
hoping I'd find more.

There has to be,
be something else,
a solid firm thing
somewhere around here.

It can't all be thin,
not all of it,
there has to be more
beyond this pit.

One day I'll finish this poem,
once I find it,
but until that day,
I'll just be